KEVIN SUPPLES

Speaking Out

The Civil Rights Movement
1950–1964

NATIONAL GEOGRAPHIC

Washington, D.C.

PICTURE CREDITS
cover (top), pages 29 (border), 32-33 (border), 36-40 (border) UCLA Fowler Museum of
Cultural History, Photo by Don Cole; cover (back) Robert Parent/TimePix; cover (left), pages
20, 31 (top), 40 Flip Schulke/CORBIS; cover (right) Khue Bui/AP Photo; page 3 (right)
Stockphoto; page 1 (right) Howard Sochurek/Timepix; pages 1 (left), 3 (second from right),
3 (left), 7 (background), 9, 19 CORBIS; pages 1 (frames), 2-7 (border), 13-19 (border), 21-
27 (border) detail-Newark Museum of Art/Art Resource, NY; page 2 bob Adelman/Magnum
Photos; page 3 (second from left) Reuters New Media Inc./CORBIS; page 4 Courtesy of
Library of Congress; page 5 Hulton-Archive/Getty Images; page 6 The Schomburg Center
for Research in Black Culture, New York Public Library; page 7 (top left), 7 (bottom right)
National Portrait Gallery, Smithsonian Institution/Art Resource, NY; pages 8, 10 (left), 10
(right), 11 (top), 13, 17, 18, 21 (top), 22, 23 (left middle, left bottom, and right), 26, 28, 30-
31, 35 (top), 38 Bettmann/CORBIS; pages 9-11 (border) Lonely Planet Images; pages 11
(bottom), 21 (bottom), 32 David J. & Janice L. Frent Collection/ CORBIS; pages 14, 15 Carl
Iwasaki/TimePix; pages 16, 24, 27 (bottom), 29, 30 (top), 31 (bottom), 35 (bottom)
AP/Wide World Photos; page 23 (top left) Gene Herrick/AP/Wide World Photos; page 25
(background) Grey Villet/TimePix; page 25 (bottom) Time Magazine, Inc./TimePix; page 27
(top) Jack Moebes/CORBIS; page 30 (bottom) Charles Moore/Black Star/TimePix; page 33
Eve Arnold/Magnum Photos; page 34 (top) Nobel Foundation/CorbisSygma; page34
(bottom) Steve Schapiro/BlackStar/ Stockphoto page 36-37 Wally McNamee/CORBIS; page
37 Francis Miller/TimePix.

Library of Congress Cataloging-in-Publication Data

Supples, Kevin.
  Speaking out : the Civil Rights Movement, 1950-1964 / by Kevin Supples.
    v. cm. — (Crossroads America)
Contents: America in 1950 — Free but not equal — The movement begins— The
struggle continues — Crisis in the movement. 1. Civil rights movements—United
States—History—20th century—Juvenile literature. 2. African Americans—Civil
rights—History—20th century—Juvenile literature. 3. African Americans—History—
1877–1964—Juvenile literature. [1. Civil rights movements. 2. African Americans--Civil
rights. 3. Race relations.] I. Title. II. Series.
  E185.61.S945 2006
  323.1'196073'009045—dc22
                           2003019828

ISBN: 0-7922-8279-5
Library Edition ISBN: 0-7922-8359-7

Produced through the worldwide resources of the National Geographic Society, John M.
Fahey, Jr., President and Chief Executive Officer; Gilbert M. Grosvenor, Chairman of the
Board; Nina D. Hoffman, Executive Vice President and President, Books and School
Publishing.

PREPARED BY NATIONAL GEOGRAPHIC SCHOOL PUBLISHING
Ericka Markman, President, Children's Books & Educational Publishing Group; Steve Mico,
Senior Vice President & Editorial Director; Marianne Hiland, Editorial Manager; Anita
Schwartz, Project Editor; Tara Peterson, Sam England, Editorial Assistants; Jim Hiscott,
Design Manager; Linda McKnight, Art Director; Diana Bourdrez, Anne Whittle, Photo
Research; Matt Wascavage, Manager of Publishing Services; Sean Philpotts, Production
Coordinator; Jane Ponton, Production Artist; Susan Kehnemui Donnelly, Children's Books
Project Editor. Production; Clifton M. Brown III, Manufacturing and Quality Control.

PROGRAM DEVELOPMENT
Gare Thompson Associates, Inc.

BOOK DEVELOPMENT—Thomas Nieman, Inc.

CONSULTANT/REVIEWER—Dr. Margit E. McGuire, School of Education, Seattle University,
Seattle, Washington
Dr. Russell L. Adams, Professor and Chair, Afro-American Studies, Howard University

BOOK DESIGN—Steven Curtis Design, Inc.

NATIONAL GEOGRAPHIC SOCIETY
1145 17th Street, N.W.
Washington, D.C. 20036-4688

Printed in Mexico.

Table of Contents

Thurgood Marshall   Rosa Parks   Martin Luther King, Jr.   Malcolm X

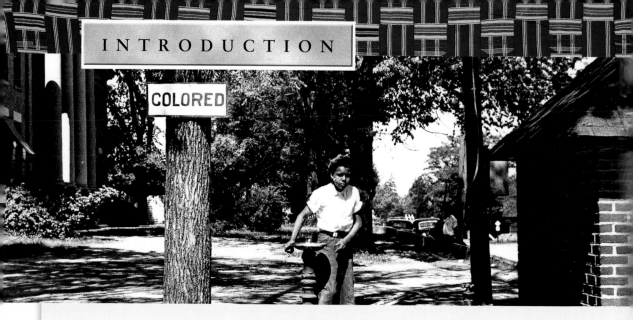

America in 1950

A DIVIDED SOCIETY

*T*he 1950s were good years for many Americans. They had jobs that paid well, new homes in the suburbs, good schools for their children. But African Americans were one group who did not share fully in all this. In the 1950s, **prejudice** against African Americans was widespread in the United States. One of the worst results of this hatred was **segregation**, the separation of people based on race.

Segregation was different in different parts of the United States. The South was home to more than half of African Americans. In the South, segregation was enforced by **Jim Crow laws**. These laws had controlled the lives of Southern blacks since the late 1800s. Jim Crow laws said that blacks and whites must use different schools, restaurants, hotels, theaters, parks, different sections of trains and buses, and so on.

Even funeral homes and cemeteries were segregated! In the few places where blacks and whites shared public services—such as post offices and banks—African Americans had to wait for all whites to be served first.

In the North, segregation was enforced by practice and custom. Many African Americans moved to Northern cities during the 1940s. Whites responded by moving to the suburbs. African Americans found themselves trapped in city slums, poor neighborhoods where housing and schools were bad and there were few jobs.

Both Northern and Southern segregation were wrong. Both forms denied black people an equality that they had a right to as Americans. In the 1950s, some African Americans were determined to change things. They started the Civil Rights Movement.

IN THEIR OWN WORDS

" If you're born in America with a black skin, you're born in prison. "

Malcolm X

5

THE ROOTS OF THE MOVEMENT

*T*he Civil Rights Movement of the 1950s and 1960s really started in the early 1900s. In 1909, a group of African-American and white reformers founded the **NAACP**, the National Association for the Advancement of Colored People. Its founders included black leaders such as W. E. B. Du Bois and Ida B. Wells-Barnett.

The chief goal of the NAACP was to win equal rights for African Americans. It helped blacks to register to vote. NAACP lawyers used the courts to protect African-American rights. It fought hate crimes against blacks, such as **lynching**. The NAACP grew from a small group to a powerful force. In 1914, it had about 6,000 members. By 1920, over 90 thousand people belonged to the NAACP.

The United States suffered through hard times in the 1930s. One out of every four American workers was unemployed. But the jobless rate for African Americans was much worse.

In some Northern cities, more than half of the black men were out of work. And joblessness among black women was even higher. Many of these unemployed African Americans found jobs in federal government projects.

During these years, African-American leaders had some successes. They used the federal government to attack segregation and increase opportunities for blacks. A few black leaders served in the federal government under President Franklin D. Roosevelt. They were members of a group that advised him on racial issues. One of the most important of these black leaders was Mary McLeod Bethune. She headed a government agency that helped give job training to young African Americans.

NAACP MARCH AGAINST LYNCHING

W. E. B. DU BOIS

AFRICAN AMERICAN
WORKING ON A
GOVERNMENT ROAD-
BUILDING PROJECT

MARY MCLEOD
BETHUNE

COLORED
WAITING ROOM
INTRASTATE PASSENGERS →

← PULLMAN PASSENGERS
CHECK WITH PULLMAN
CONDUCTOR AT RECEIVING
TABLE BEFORE GOING TO
TRAINS 4-11-&-36
CARS A-43-54-47&5-58

AFRICAN-AMERICAN
SOLDIERS RETURNED
TO FIND SEGREGATION
UNCHANGED.

CHAPTER 1

Free but Not Equal

AFRICAN-AMERICAN DEFENSE WORKER

WORLD WAR II

*T*he United States entered World War II in December 1941. During the war years, African Americans worked for their rights while serving their country. The slogan was "Victory at Home and Victory Abroad."

In early 1941, African-American labor leader A. Philip Randolph planned a huge march on Washington. He wanted the federal government to force factories that made equipment for the armed forces to hire more black workers. The threat of the march caused President Roosevelt to issue an order ending segregation in defense factories and government offices. Over a million African Americans worked in defense factories during World War II.

Nearly one million black men and women served in the American armed forces during the war. Many believed that fighting for their country would help them become equal citizens with equal rights. It didn't.

Black soldiers and white soldiers lived in separate buildings. They even had separate recreation areas. But African-American soldiers found a different world in Europe. There, blacks and whites mixed in restaurants, theaters, and neighborhoods. African Americans found coming home to a segregated society very difficult to accept.

IN THEIR OWN WORDS

"Freedom is never granted; it is won."

A. Philip Randolph

PROGRESS AND PROBLEMS

From 1900 to 1950, most African Americans lived in the South. During this period, there were two large-scale movements north by blacks. The first took place between 1915 and 1930. The second started during World War II, as Southern blacks took jobs in Northern factories to help the war effort.

Blacks found better jobs and schools in the North. And because large numbers of blacks were crowding into big Northern cities, their voting power became greater. African Americans helped elect black candidates.

Blacks also faced big problems in the North. In crowded Northern cities, blacks often found it difficult to get good housing. Segregation forced them into slum neighborhoods. African Americans also faced the threat of racial violence. In the summer of 1943, there were race riots in a number of American cities.

RIOTERS RUN FROM POLICE DURING A RACE RIOT

EARLY IN 1949, AFRICAN-AMERICAN MEMBERS OF CONGRESS WILLIAM L. DAWSON (LEFT) AND ADAM CLAYTON POWELL STANDING NEAR THE CAPITOL IN WASHINGTON, D.C.

From the founding of the NAACP, the goals of African-American reformers had been to end segregation and to gain equal rights for black citizens. They wanted **integration**. This meant allowing people from different racial and ethnic backgrounds to share freely in all areas of American society. The first steps in this direction were taken just after the war.

Until the mid-1940s, major league baseball was a whites-only sport. Then in October 1945, Branch Rickey, the owner and manager of the Brooklyn Dodgers, signed African-American star Jackie Robinson to play for the Montreal Royals, a Brooklyn farm team. Two years later, Robinson was brought up to the Dodgers.

Many players and fans were bitterly opposed to integrating baseball. But Robinson showed great courage in facing all kinds of abuse. In his first year in the majors, he won the Rookie of the Year Award. Baseball's color line was shattered. Other black baseball players soon followed Robinson into the major leagues.

ROOKIE OF THE YEAR
19 47
JACKIE ROBINSON

IN THEIR OWN WORDS

" African Americans want to make the dream of America become flesh and blood, bread and butter, freedom and equality. "

Adam Clayton Powell

11

THURGOOD MARSHALL

CHAPTER 2

The Movement Begins

FIGHTER FOR CIVIL RIGHTS

MARSHALL IN FRONT OF
THE SUPREME COURT

*T*he leader of the NAACP's efforts to end segregation was their top lawyer, Thurgood Marshall. He used the law to fight injustice against African Americans. Marshall argued 32 cases before the U.S. **Supreme Court** during his career. He won 29 of them. Some say that Marshall did more than anyone else to win civil rights for African Americans.

Marshall was born in Maryland in 1908. He was raised in a proud middle-class family. Smart and hard-working, he was a fine student. Marshall went to college and later attended law school at Howard University, in Washington, D.C. Marshall graduated in 1933, first in his class. In his first big case, he fought to have the University of Maryland Law School accept its first black student. Marshall won his case.

Most of Marshall's clients were poor people. Some couldn't pay anything. Marshall worked hard for them anyway. He usually won his cases. He became known as the "little man's lawyer." Marshall had a good sense of humor. He enjoyed jokes and often used humor to help him get through hard times.

IN THEIR OWN WORDS

" A child born to a black mother in a state like Mississippi has exactly the same rights as a white baby born to the wealthiest person in the United States. It's not true, but I challenge anyone to say it is not a goal worth working for. "

Thurgood Marshall

"SEPARATE BUT EQUAL"

Throughout his career, Thurgood Marshall fought the "separate-but-equal" rule. This rule was created in 1896 by the Supreme Court. It said that states could offer separate services to African Americans and whites as long as the services were about equal. But in most cases they weren't.

Many states passed laws saying that local school districts could decide whether to have separate schools for blacks and whites. The result was that all schools in the South were segregated. And there was nothing "equal" about the education black children were given in their poor, crowded schools.

After World War II, many Southern states tried to improve their blacks-only schools. They wanted to show that these schools were equal. But their efforts were too little and too late. By 1952, there were several court cases about segregated schools. The most famous involved an eight-year-old girl named Linda Brown.

Linda's family lived close to a public school in Topeka, Kansas. But that school accepted only white students. So Linda had to travel by bus to a blacks-only school. To reach their bus stop, she and her sister had to walk through a dangerous railroad yard. Early in 1951, the Browns and some other African-American families decided to take the local school district to court. In July, the local school board promised they would end segregation "as soon as possible." But that wasn't good enough for the Browns.

LINDA BROWN AND HER SISTER WALKING TO THEIR BUS STOP

" *Equal* means getting the same thing at the same time and in the same place. "

Thurgood Marshall

LINDA BROWN (LOWER RIGHT) IN SEGREGATED CLASSROOM

BROWN V. BOARD OF EDUCATION

The Browns' case became famous. Thurgood Marshall decided to use it to try to end segregated schools everywhere. As head of the NAACP's legal team, he brought the case to the Supreme Court. The court decided to group the Browns' case with four others. Their case is known as *Brown v. Board of Education.*

Marshall argued the case before the Supreme Court. He argued that the Fourteenth Amendment of the U.S. Constitution said that states must treat all citizens alike, regardless of race. He said that black children did not receive schooling equal to that given white children. He also said that black children thought less of themselves because they attended poor schools.

Almost three years after Linda Brown's family first started the case, a final decision was reached. On May 17, 1954, the Supreme Court ruled that school segregation went against the Constitution.

After the ruling, the government made many school districts redraw their borders. Now white and black students would go to school together. This victory was an important step in the fight for civil rights. Many hoped that integrating schools would lead to integrating all of society. But there was still a long struggle ahead.

HAPPY NAACP LAWYERS (LEFT TO RIGHT) GEORGE E. C. HAYES, THURGOOD MARSHALL, AND JAMES M. NABRIT FOLLOWING THEIR VICTORY IN LINDA BROWN'S CASE

"We conclude that in the field of public education, the doctrine of 'separate but equal' has no place."

Chief Justice Earl Warren, in the Brown *case*

The News
Greater Washington Edition

HIGH COURT BANS SEGREGATION IN PUBLIC SCHOOLS

A WOMAN EXPLAINING THE MEANING OF THE SUPREME COURT DECISION TO HER DAUGHTER

17

ELIZABETH ECKFORD WALKING
BY JEERING WHITE CLASSMATES

IN THEIR OWN WORDS

"In the course of our country's progress toward equality of opportunity, you have shown dignity and courage in circumstances which would daunt citizens of lesser faith."

President Dwight Eisenhower, telegram to the parents of the Little Rock Nine

THE LITTLE ROCK NINE

Within a year, some school districts desegregated. Here and there, African-American and white students attended school together. But many school districts, especially in the South, found ways to resist and delay the Supreme Court ruling.

Little Rock, Arkansas, became a test case for the new ruling. Public schools there were ordered to desegregate in September 1957. The local school board agreed. But the governor of Arkansas, Orval Faubus, refused. He was facing a tough re-election fight. He hoped to win the support of the many white Arkansas voters who still wanted segregated schools.

When school opened that September, Governor Faubus sent National Guard troops to Central High School. He ordered them to stop nine African-American students from entering the newly integrated school. Elizabeth Eckford, one of the "Little Rock Nine," arrived at school alone. A white mob screamed abuse at her.

For three weeks, the crisis continued. At this point, President Dwight Eisenhower stepped in. He placed the Arkansas National Guard under federal control. The nine black students arrived at the school in a U.S. Army car. With soldiers protecting them, the students finally integrated the school. Eisenhower had shown that the federal government would protect civil rights.

NATIONAL GUARD TROOPS STAND OUTSIDE CENTRAL HIGH SCHOOL.

"Oppressed people cannot remain oppressed forever. The urge for freedom will eventually come."

Martin Luther King, Jr.

CHAPTER 3

The Struggle Continues

MARTIN LUTHER KING, JR., AND HIS WIFE, CORETTA SCOTT KING

A NEW LEADER

*T*he legal victory of Brown *v.* Board of Education *was just one step in the fight against segregation.* It did not change things as quickly as people had hoped. So, African Americans began to organize. They were ready to do more. Then a new leader arrived at this moment in history. He was a young minister named Martin Luther King, Jr.

King was born in 1929 in Atlanta, Georgia, to a middle-class family. He was the son and grandson of Baptist ministers. His mother was a teacher. One of his grandfathers had been a slave. King excelled at school. He began college at the age of 15 in a program for gifted students. He went to Morehouse College, a well-known all-black school in Atlanta. By the time King was 18, he had decided to follow in his father's footsteps.

While at Boston University finishing his studies to be a minister, King met Coretta Scott. She was studying voice and piano. The two were married in 1953. The following year, Reverend King became pastor of a church in Montgomery, Alabama. He quickly became known for his wisdom and powerful preaching. Then in December 1955, an event took place that would make Martin Luther King, Jr., a leader of the Civil Rights Movement.

ROSA PARKS

Montgomery, Alabama, was a segregated city in 1955. African Americans were treated as second-class citizens there. The public bus system was a constant reminder of this.

As in many Southern cities, more blacks rode the city buses than whites. Even so, the first ten rows of every bus were reserved for white passengers only. If a bus was crowded and a white passenger needed a seat, blacks had to stand. Black passengers had to pay their fares at the front of the bus. But then they had to get off the bus and re-board by the back door. At busy times, the bus sometimes left before everyone who had paid got on.

On December 1, 1955, Rosa Parks was riding the bus home from work. She was a seamstress. She also worked at the local NAACP office. Parks had been on her feet all day, and she was tired. She was sitting in the 11th row—the first row of seats set aside for African-American passengers.

The bus was crowded. Some black passengers were standing at the back. When a white man needed a seat, the bus driver ordered Parks and three African Americans in her row to stand. She refused to move. Parks was taken off the bus, arrested, and put in a jail cell.

ROSA PARKS WALKING TO JAIL

IN THEIR OWN WORDS

" When the driver saw that I was still sitting there, he asked if I was going to stand up. I told him, no, I wasn't. He said, 'Well, if you don't stand up, I'm going to have you arrested.' I told him to go on and have me arrested. "

Rosa Parks

PARKS
BEING
FINGERPRINTED

PARKS LEAVING
WITH HER LAWYER

ROSA
PARKS

PARKS TALKING
TO A REPORTER

THE MONTGOMERY BUS BOYCOTT

News of Parks's arrest shocked the African-American community. Civil rights supporters saw that this was their chance to change the rules. They asked Martin Luther King, Jr., to be their leader. That evening, Dr. King spoke to a cheering crowd of African Americans. He called for them to start a bus **boycott,** which meant they would not ride the buses.

For the next year, very few African Americans rode a public bus in Montgomery, Alabama. Most used carpools to get to work. The boycott worked. The bus company lost a lot of money.

Then in June 1956, a federal court ruled that the bus segregation in Alabama was against the Constitution. The city of Montgomery did not give in easily. Lawyers for the city took the case to the Supreme Court. But that November, the Supreme Court agreed that segregation on buses was not lawful. A little over a year after the day that Rosa Parks refused to move, the Montgomery buses were integrated.

The Montgomery bus boycott was big news. It made Martin Luther King, Jr., famous. *Time* magazine put him on its cover. Requests to speak poured in from all over the country. The publicity led to boycotts in many other parts of the South.

A NEARLY EMPTY BUS SHOWS THE EFFECT OF THE BOYCOTT

AFRICAN AMERICANS WALKING
TO WORK DURING THE
MONTGOMERY BUS BOYCOTT

FEBRUARY 18, 1957

TWENTY CENTS

TIME
THE WEEKLY NEWSMAGAZINE

Montgomery, Alabama's
REV. MARTIN LUTHER KING

VOL. LXIX NO. 7

$7.00 A YEAR

25

SIT-INS

In February 1960, four African-American college freshmen in Greensboro, North Carolina, decided to take another step toward equality. They sat down at the whites-only lunch counter in a Woolworth's store and politely ordered coffee and doughnuts. The students were refused service. At that time, many department stores across the country had lunch counters. But Southern lunch counters did not serve African Americans. Blacks were free to shop at the stores but could not eat there.

In protest, the four students sat at the counter for the rest of the afternoon. They returned the next day. This time, 20 more students came with them. Each day, more people—both black and white—joined the "sit-in." By Saturday, hundreds jammed the lunch counters.

The events in Greensboro became news. At first, white business leaders refused to bend to the protest. But then black citizens set up a boycott of local stores. Stores began losing money. Finally, on July 25, 1960, the first black person was served lunch at Woolworth's.

During the next 18 months, thousands of people staged sit-ins all over the South. Most of those taking part were black students. Both Martin Luther King, Jr., and Thurgood Marshall supported these nonviolent protests. African Americans had found a new and powerful way to be heard.

In the fall of 1960, John F. Kennedy was elected president of the United States. Kennedy won 70 percent of the black vote. He had shown that he would support ending segregation. Kennedy did not make changes quickly. But he did appoint more African Americans to high federal positions than any president before him. Kennedy appointed Thurgood Marshall to be a federal judge.

JOHN F. KENNEDY

AFRICAN-AMERICAN STUDENTS IN GREENSBORO STAGING THE FIRST LUNCH COUNTER SIT-IN

WHITES ATTACKING SIT-IN PROTESTERS AT A LUNCH COUNTER IN JACKSON, MISSISSIPPI

MARTIN LUTHER KING, JR., IN
A JAIL CELL IN BIRMINGHAM

28

CHAPTER 4

Crisis in the Movement

AFRICAN AMERICANS
BEING SPRAYED WITH
FIRE HOSES DURING
PROTESTS IN BIRMINGHAM

BIRMINGHAM, 1963

*I*n April 1963, Coretta Scott King called President Kennedy. Her husband had been jailed the day before. She wanted the president's help. Martin Luther King, Jr., had been working with citizens fighting for their rights in Birmingham, Alabama.

Civil rights workers staged boycotts, marches, and sit-ins. They were working to register black voters. A local police official, Eugene "Bull" Connor, had ordered all protests stopped. But led by Reverend King, the civil rights workers continued. He and others were then arrested and put in jail.

News of King's arrest helped fuel more protests. Thousands of students and children, some as young as six years old, joined in a "children's crusade."

On May 3, the police used dogs, clubs, and high-powered fire hoses against the protesters. Angry marchers threw rocks and bottles at the police. Thousands were jailed.

On May 10, city leaders agreed to desegregate. Many whites refused to accept this. Bombs rocked a black-owned motel and the home of King's brother. Angry, blacks began to riot. It was getting harder for them to keep their protests nonviolent.

IN THEIR OWN WORDS

> **"**There comes a time when people get tired . . . of being kicked about by the brutal feet of oppression.**"**
>
> *Martin Luther King, Jr.*

29

News Photographs

Most Americans experienced the civil rights struggle through pictures in newspapers and magazines and, especially, on television. Many reacted with horror to what they saw. Millions of Americans came to support the protesters. They put pressure on lawmakers to make real changes.

POLICE USING DOGS AGAINST CIVIL RIGHTS PROTESTERS IN BIRMINGHAM IN THE SUMMER OF 1963

FIREHOSES BEING USED AGAINST BIRMINGHAM PROTESTERS IN 1963

MYRLIE EVERS AT THE
FUNERAL OF HER HUSBAND,
CIVIL RIGHTS LEADER
MEDGAR EVERS, WHO WAS
MURDERED IN MISSISSIPPI
IN JUNE 1963

BUS CARRYING "FREEDOM RIDERS"
THAT WAS FIREBOMBED BY WHITES
IN ALABAMA IN MAY 1961

FOUR LITTLE GIRLS MURDERED IN THE BOMBING
OF A BIRMINGHAM CHURCH IN SEPTEMBER 1963

MALCOLM X

Most African Americans shared Martin Luther King's belief in nonviolence. But one black leader had a very different philosophy. Malcolm X rejected integration. He wanted to create a separate black nation. He supported armed self-defense. And he encouraged blacks to take pride in their own culture and history.

Malcolm X was born Malcolm Little in Omaha, Nebraska, on May 19, 1925. He was one of eight children. His father was a Baptist preacher. A white hate group drove the family out of town. Another hate group burned down their new home in Michigan. Soon after, his father was killed. The children were sent to foster homes. Malcolm quit school in the eighth grade, when a teacher suggested that he give up his dream of law school to become a carpenter. Malcolm moved to New York City and turned to crime. Before his 21st birthday, he was sent to jail for six years.

Malcolm's life changed in jail. He spent every moment reading. He also became a powerful speaker. He decided to devote himself to helping African Americans. Once out of prison, he gave many speeches. He spoke to college students and on city street corners. He became the symbol for what was later known as **Black Power**. This was the movement of African Americans to win control of their own communities.

"We are not fighting for integration, nor are we fighting for separation. We are fighting for recognition as human beings."

Malcolm X

A BODYGUARD PROTECTS MALCOLM X AT A RALLY. THE BLACK LEADER WAS MURDERED BY POLITICAL OPPONENTS IN FEBRUARY 1965.

How Should African Americans Win Their Rights?

In the 1960s, Martin Luther King, Jr., and Malcolm X came to stand for opposite points of view on how African Americans should win their civil rights.

Martin Luther King, Jr., stressed nonviolent methods. Although King himself was jailed and his own home was bombed, he begged civil rights supporters not to fight back. Soon, his ideas about nonviolent protest became one of the main features of the civil rights movement.

In the process of gaining our rightful place, we must not be guilty of wrongful deeds. Let us not seek to satisfy our thirst for freedom by drinking from the cup of bitterness and hatred.

If cursed, do not curse back. If pushed, do not push back. If struck, do not strike back.

Hate cannot drive out hate; only love can do that.

AFRICAN-AMERICAN AND WHITE CIVIL RIGHTS WORKERS SINGING TOGETHER IN 1964

Malcolm X became impatient with King's nonviolent strategy. He had his own ideas for how to win the long-running black struggle.

U.S. ATHLETES TOMMIE SMITH (CENTER) AND JOHN CARLOS (RIGHT) GIVE BLACK POWER SALUTES AFTER THEIR VICTORIES IN THE SUMMER OLYMPICS IN 1968.

Nonviolence is the philosophy of a fool. There is no philosophy more befitting to the white man's tactics for keeping his foot on the black man's neck.

You get freedom by letting your enemy know that you'll do anything to get your freedom; then you'll get it. It's the only way you'll get it.

I don't have any hate. I've got some sense. I'm not going to let somebody who hates me tell me to love him.

Malcolm X was murdered by three black men in 1965; Martin Luther King, Jr., was murdered by a white man in 1968. Both men were only 39 at the time they died. Despite their early deaths, the ideas of both leaders continued to influence the Civil Rights Movement.

"I HAVE A DREAM"

In June 1963, President Kennedy demanded that Congress pass a strong civil rights bill. In a speech to the nation he asked, "Are we to say to the world—and much more importantly to each other,—that this is the land of the free, except for the Negroes?"

To persuade Congress to pass the bill, civil rights leaders A. Philip Randolph and Bayard Rustin organized a huge march on Washington, D.C. On August 28, more than 250,000 people—both African Americans and whites—came together in the nation's capital. Labor unions and religious leaders joined the protest.

MARTIN LUTHER KING, JR., AT THE MARCH ON WASHINGTON

It was the largest show of support for the civil rights movement so far. The march ended at the Lincoln Memorial. For three hours, the crowd listened to a lot of speeches. People were getting sleepy and restless when the last speaker, Martin Luther King, Jr., came to the microphone. His famous "I Have a Dream" speech electrified the crowd.

A few months after the March on Washington, President Kennedy was assassinated. His vice-president, Lyndon Johnson, succeeded him. President Johnson passed the **Civil Rights Act of 1964**. The new law banned segregation in public places. It also banned unfair treatment of workers based on their color, sex, religion, or national origin.

IN THEIR OWN WORDS

"I have a dream that my four little children will one day live in a nation where they will not be judged by the color of their skin, but by the content of their character."

Martin Luther King, Jr.

Legacy

The Civil Rights Movement had important successes. It ended segregation based on Jim Crow laws. It greatly increased the number of African-American voters. And as more blacks were able to vote, more blacks were elected to political office. The movement also gave African Americans a greater sense of pride in who they were and what blacks had contributed to American history and culture.

But in the years following the March on Washington, the Civil Rights Movement also faced difficult challenges. Many blacks became angry at the slow pace of change. Violence based on race hatred continued. African Americans were still struggling with unfair treatment in housing, education, and jobs. But the effort to make Martin Luther King's dream a reality went on.

Glossary

BLACK POWER movement of African Americans to win control of their own communities

BOYCOTT a protest in which people refuse to buy or use something

BROWN v. BOARD OF EDUCATION 1954 ruling by the U.S. Supreme Court that outlawed segregation in the public schools

CIVIL RIGHTS ACT OF 1964 law that banned segregation in public places. It also banned unfair treatment of workers based on their color, sex, religion, or national origin

INTEGRATION putting together (in schools, workplaces, and so on) people from different races

JIM CROW LAWS laws that said that African Americans and whites must use different schools, restaurants, hotels, theaters, parks, and so on

LYNCHING putting a person to death, usually by hanging, without a lawful trial

NAACP National Association for the Advancement of Colored People, an organization founded in 1909 to advance the legal and political rights of African Americans

PREJUDICE hatred of a particular race, religion, or group

SEGREGATION separation of people, often by race

"SEPARATE BUT EQUAL" rule created in 1896 by the Supreme Court that allowed states to offer separate services to blacks and whites as long as the services were about equal

SIT-IN nonviolent protest in which people sit down in a public place and refuse to move until their demands are met

SUPREME COURT highest federal court in the United States, with legal authority over all the other courts in the nation

Index